On Beyond a Million

Million

An Amazing Math Journey

David M. Schwartz

illustrated by Paul Meisel

BANTAM
SCHOOL
VISITORS
PARKING

A Doubleday Book
for Young Readers

For my sister, Judy,
who's one in a million
and beyond
—D.M.S.

For my dad,
who gave me an
appreciation of math
(and tennis)
—P.M.

A Doubleday Book for Young Readers
Published by Random House, Inc.
1540 Broadway, New York, New York 10036
Doubleday and the portrayal of an anchor with a dolphin
are trademarks of Random House, Inc.
Text copyright © 1999 by David Schwartz
Illustrations copyright © 1999 by Paul Meisel

Cataloging-in-Publication Data available
from the Library of Congress.
ISBN: 0-385-32217-8
The text of this book is set in 15-point One Stroke Script.
Book design by Semadar Megged
Manufactured in the United States of America
October 1999
10 9 8 7 6 5 4 3 2 1

Did you know?

The Sears Tower in Chicago is 110 stories high.

The U.S. Postal Service delivers 200 pieces of junk mail every second.

It has been 400 years since rain has fallen in the driest place on Earth, the Atacama Desert of Chile.

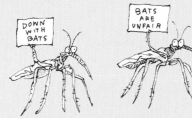

One little brown bat can snap up 600 mosquitoes per hour.

There are about 1,000 hairs on a square inch of your head.

One thousand! These numbers are getting big really fast.

This is faster than counting by tens. Faster than counting by hundreds.

That's why it's Power Counting!

It's power-ful, that's for sure!

10^2 is called ten to the second power
$10^2 = 10 \times 10 = 100$

10^3 is called ten to the third power
$10^3 = 10 \times 10 \times 10 = 1,000$

The little numbers are called exponents. An exponent tells you how many times to multiply a number by itself.

So ten multiplied by itself three times is 10^3?

Giant tortoises can weigh 500 pounds or more. During the age of sailing ships, sailors kept them in the holds, where they could survive for more than a year.

Did you know?

The oldest trees on Earth are about 2,200 years old.

To taste your food, you use 9,000 taste buds on your tongue.

There are 40,000 different characters in Chinese, while our alphabet has only 26 letters.

If all the veins in your body were stretched out in one line, they would extend 70,000 miles.

100,000 people worked 20 seasons to build one pyramid.

Did you know?

There are 400,000 hairs on a square inch of a sea otter's pelt.

One colony of weaver ants contains 500,000 ants. They weave nests out of leaves in the treetops.

If everyone in the United States recycled their newspapers, we would save 500,000 trees every week.

Up to 1,000,000 (one million) leaf-cutter ants can live in one colony. They can strip rain forests of their leaves and destroy croplands overnight.

A square yard in the rocky area of seashore between high tide and low tide may be home to 900,000 animals.

Thanks a million, Professor X. You're one in a million!

It only took us six counts!

That's because a million is 10^6. That means a one with six zeros.

A million is the same as a thousand thousand. A thousand is $10 \times 10 \times 10$, and if we multiply that by another thousand, or $10 \times 10 \times 10$, we have $10 \times 10 \times 10 \times 10 \times 10 \times 10 = 10^6 =$ One Million!

Hmmm. So $10^3 \times 10^3$ is the same as 10^6? All you have to do is add those little exponents together and you get your answer: $10^3 \times 10^3 = 10^6$. Easy!

Cool!

Did you know?

If you doubled a penny every day, after 30 days you would have a total of $10,737,418.23 (ten million, seven hundred and thirty-seven thousand, four hundred and eighteen dollars and twenty-three cents).

Every day, 37,000,000 (thirty-seven million) Tootsie Rolls come rolling out of the factory.

On your sixth birthday you have lived 189,216,000 (one hundred eighty-nine million, two hundred and sixteen thousand) seconds.

There are about 250,000,000 (two hundred fifty million) people in the United States today.

Americans eat about 500,000,000 (five hundred million) pounds of popcorn each year.

If you live an average life, your heart will beat about 2,200,000,000 (two billion, two million) times and you will live to an age of 2,400,000,000 (two billion, four million) seconds, or 76 years.

The universe contains 50,000,000,000 (fifty billion) to 100,000,000,000 (one hundred billion) galaxies. Alone, our galaxy, the Milky Way, has 100,000,000,000 (one hundred billion) to 300,000,000,000 (three hundred billion) stars.

There are about 5,000,000,000 (five billion) people alive in the world today.

ONE TRILLION!!!

A one with twelve zeros.

It's a thousand billion.

No, it's a million million.

Stop arguing, they're the same!

Is a trillion the biggest number in the whole wide world?

No.

No way!

Ten billion, one hundred billion, one trillion.

So what is the biggest number?

A TRILLION

= ONE MILLION MILLION

$$= 1,000,000,000,000$$

$$= 1,000 \times 1,000,000,000$$

$$= 1,000,000 \times 1,000,000$$

$$= 10^3 \times 10^9 = 10^{12}$$

$$= 10^6 \times 10^6 = 10^{12}$$

$$= 10 \times 10 \times 10 \times 10 \times 10 \times 10$$
$$\times 10 \times 10 \times 10 \times 10 \times 10 \times 10$$

Googol.

Centillion.

Googolplex.

Zillion.

Gazillion. Or maybe bajillion. Hmmm, which is bigger, gazillion or bajillion?

Infinity.

Did you know?

Light travels about 6,000,000,000,000 (six trillion) miles in a year. That distance is called one light-year.

There are 10,000,000,000,000,000,000,000 (ten sextillion) atoms in every breath you take.

The Earth weighs about 13,000,000,000,000,000,000,000,000 (thirteen septillion) pounds.

3×10^{72} (3 x 1,000,000,000,000,000, 000,000,000,000,000,000,000,000, 000,000,000,000,000,000,000,000, 000,000,000) is the approximate number of atoms in the universe, according to some scientists. But no one really knows.

The Sun gives off as much light as 6,000,000,000,000,000,000,000,000 (six septillion) 60-watt lightbulbs.

Quadrillion, quintillion, sextillion, septillion, octillion, nonillion, decillion . . .

Look, the numbers are growing by powers of one thousand. Each one is a thousand times bigger than the last one.

How do you say

79,538,387,920,
899,947,
478,111,348,
980,792,404,040,199,
479,138,555?

79 quindecillion,
538 quattuordecillion,
387 tredecillion,
920 duodecillion,
899 undecillion,
947 decillion,
478 nonillion,
111 octillion,
348 septillion,
980 sextillion,
792 quintillion,
404 quadrillion,
40 trillion,
199 billion,
479 million,
138 thousand,
five hundred
fifty-five.

10^{100}

is a lot easier to write than

10,000,000,000,
000,000,000,000,
000,000,000,000,
000,000,000,000,
000,000,000,000,
000,000,000,000,
000,000,000,000,
000,000,000,000,
000,000,000,000,
000,000.